The Countryside
in pictures

Pictures
to share

For Keith, who's still
climbing mountains

**Pictures
to share**

This edition published in 2013 by
Pictures to Share Community Interest Company,
a UK based social enterprise that publishes
illustrated books for older people.

www.picturestoshare.co.uk

ISBN 978-0-9563818-5-9

Front Cover: Sheep, 1877 (oil on canvas), Charles Jones (1836-92)
© Russell-Cotes Art Gallery and Museum, Bournemouth, UK
/The Bridgeman Art Library
Endpapers: Butterflies © Ann Bridges www.ann-bridges.com
Title page: Berry Garland by Jan Kerton.
From A-Z of Stumpwork/Country Bumkin Publications,
Australia www.countrybumkin.com.au

The Countryside
in pictures

Edited by Helen J Bate

What a
glorious morning
is this.

Quotation: Samuel Adams (1722-1803)

Painting: Cockerel © Mary Ann Rogers www.marogers.com

Thatching

is a traditional craft
dating back
over 4,000 years.

Each newly thatched
roof will last about
30 years.

Thatch can be made
of straw, water reed,
sedge, rushes
or heather.

Come we to the summer,

to the summer we will come,

For the woods are full of bluebells
and the hedges full of bloom,

And the crow is on the oak
a-building of her nest,

And love is burning diamonds
in my true lover's breast;

Quotation from 'Summer' by John Clare (1793 -1864)

Main photograph: English beech forest by Rosemary Calvert.
The Image Bank/Getty Images

Stolen sweets are always sweeter;

Stolen kisses much completer;
Stolen looks are nice in chapels,
Stolen, stolen, be your apples.

Quotation from 'Songs of Fairies Robbing an Orchard'
1830 by James Henry Leigh Hunt (1784-1859)

Main photograph: Fruit Pickers by Reg Speller. Hulton Archive/Getty Images
Small photograph: Apple core © John Farrow

If you can
catch a hare

and look into its eye
you will see the whole world.

Quotation from 'A Calendar of Hares' by Anna Crowe
From A Secret History of Rhubarb, published by Mariscat Press, Glasow
Photographs: Hare © Mike Roberts

Cheshire cheese

is naturally bright
and white in colour.

It has a crumbly texture
and a mild, milky taste.

It was produced by hand
in many farmhouses
across Cheshire during
the 20th century.

Main photograph: Cheesemaking at Beeston Hall Farm in Cheshire, 1950's
Courtesy of Peckforton Hills Local Heritage Project
Small photograph: Mouse © Emilia Stasiak istockphoto

I meant to do my work today

But a brown bird sang in the apple tree,
And a butterfly flitted across a field,
And all the leaves were calling me.

And the wind went sighing over the land
Tossing the grasses to and fro,
And a rainbow held out its shining hand
So what could I do but laugh and go?

Quotation from 'I Meant to Do My Work Today'
by Richard LeGallienne. Reprinted by permission
of The Society of Authors/Estate of Richard LeGallienne

Photograph by Grant Dixon. Lonely Planet Images/Getty Images

I will hold
my house
in the high wood

Within a walk of the sea,
And the men that were boys
when I was a boy
Shall sit and drink with me.

Quotation: from 'The South Country' from Complete Verse by Hilaire Belloc (1870 - 1953)
© The Estate of Hilaire Belloc 1970 reproduced by permission of PFD (www.pfd.co.uk)
on behalf of the Estate of Hilaire Belloc.

Photographs: Boy with dead rabbits. Photographer unknown.
Museum of English Rural Life, The University of Reading. www.reading.ac.uk/Instits/im/

18

Dancing around
a maypole

is an ancient tradition
that takes place in many countries.
In the UK maypoles are often
garlanded with greenery or flowers
and hung with long ribbons.

The ribbons are woven
around the pole
by the dancers,
forming complex patterns.

A Country Wedding

As the newly married pair left the church
to the strains of the wedding march
and the pealing of the church bells,
they passed beneath a magnificent archway,
formed by the wands of schoolgirls.

There was a large crowd of well-wishers,
and led by the village schoolboys
who were lined up on the green,
they cheered heartily.

On leaving the church,
the youngest scholar, Dorothy Hopley,
gracefully strewed the path to the road
with yellow flowers.

Wedding gifts included
a pearl and diamond pendant
from the estate tenants,
and a silver tea caddy
from the indoor and outdoor servants
at Bolesworth Castle.

Quotation: Newspaper cutting reporting the wedding
of Eleanor Barbour at Harthill Church, Cheshire, 1910

Painting: A Country Wedding by Judy Joel.
The Bridgeman Art Library/Getty Images
Small flower photographs: © Margaret Eros

Deer © Mike Jones www.mikejones-wildlife.com

Fox © Mike Jones www.mikejones-wildlife.com

In all things of nature there is something of the marvelous.

Quotation: Aristotle

Main photograph: Two children playing by a stream in the Scottish countryside around the River Clyde.
Picture Post pub 1954 © Bert Hardy/Hulton Archive/Getty Images
Small photograph: stones © Mafaldita. istockphoto

Everyone has a talent at twenty-five.

The difficult thing is to have it at fifty.

Quotation: Edgar Degas (1834 - 1917)

Photographs: Riding instructor by Reg Speller.
Hulton Archive/Getty Images

36

Life
is
one
long
process
of
getting
tired...

Quotation: Samuel Butler 1835 - 1902 English author

Picture: The Wayfarer, 1881 (oil on canvas), Edward Arthur Walton (1860-1922) / Private Collection / Photo © The Fine Art Society, London, UK / The Bridgeman Art Library

A bird
in the hand

is worth two
in the bush.

Quotation: Traditional saying

Main photograph: Christmas Is Coming by William Vanderson.
Hulton Archive/Getty Images

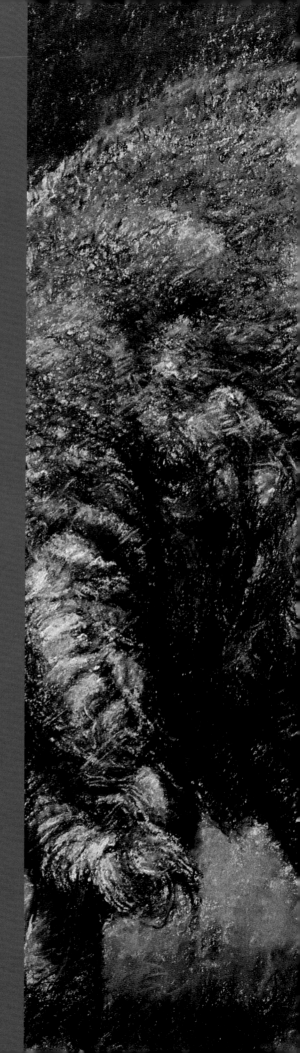

A flock of sheep that leisurely pass by,

One after one;
the sound of rain and bees

Murmuring; the fall of rivers,
winds and seas,

Smooth fields, white sheets
of water, and pure sky;

I've thought of all by turns,
and still I lie

Sleepless.

Quotation from 'To Sleep'
by William Wordsworth (1770 - 1850)

Pastel painting: 'The First Suckle'
© 1991 Keith Bowen from 'Snowdon Shepherd'
Published by Pavilion Books Ltd, London.

40

Recipe for Elderflower Cordial

It is best to pick the flowers early on a sunny day.

Ingredients

20 elderflower heads
2½ pints boiling water
3½ lbs sugar
1 sliced lemon
Citric acid (available from the chemist)

Method

Put all the dry ingredients into a clean pan
and pour boiling water over them.
Stir until sugar is dissolved.
Skim off the surface scum.
Cover with a cloth or lid.
Stir twice daily for five days.
Strain through a muslin and put in clean bottles.

For my ways are strange ways

and new ways and old ways,

And deep ways and steep ways
and high ways and low;

I'm at home and at ease
on a track that I know not,

And restless and lost
on a road that I know.

Quotation: From The Wander-Light 1902 Henry Lawson 1867-1922 Australian poet

Main photograph: Aerial view. © Andrew Holt/Photographer's Choice/Getty Images
Small photograph: compass © Dimedrol68 istockphoto

The woods are lovely, dark and deep.

But I have promises to keep,
And miles to go before I sleep.
And miles to go before I sleep.

Quotation from 'Stopping by Woods on a Snowy Evening'
by Robert Frost (1875 - 1963)

Main photograph: Sunbeams in Forest by © iStockphoto.com/AVTG.
Small photograph: Mice © Steve McWilliam (rECOrd. Chester)

Pictures to share

Acknowledgements

Our thanks to the contributors who have allowed their text or imagery to be used for a reduced or no fee.

All effort has been made to contact copyright holders. If you own the copyright for work that is represented, but have not been contacted, please get in touch via our website.

Some quotations have been provided by 'Chambers Dictionary of Quotations', Chambers Harrap Publishers Ltd, 2005

Published by
Pictures to Share Community Interest Company.
www.picturestoshare.co.uk

Graphics by Duncan Watts

Printed in England by
Langham Press, Station Road, Foxton
Cambridgeshire CB22 6SA

To see our other titles go to
www.picturestoshare.co.uk